KEY WEST
DOS & DON'TS

100 WAYS TO
LOOK LIKE A LOCAL

Enjoy!
Mandy Miles

By
Mandy Miles

Other books by Mandy Miles:

"The Best of Mandy Miles' Tan Lines"

"Only in Key West: More of Mandy Miles' Tan Lines"

Cover photo by Rob O'Neal / roboneal.com
Cover design by Dannielle Larrabee

**Don't get voted off the island!
Learn the methods to our madness.**

Mandy Miles' "Key West Dos and Don'ts"
offers a quick and hilarious crash course
on local life in a tourist town.

A longtime Key West author and newspaper
columnist, Miles offers tropical tips and island
etiquette on everything from parking and partying;
to scooter horns and Hemingway.

"In my nearly 20 years here,
no one has ever wanted to know,
'Where do the tourists go?'
But they all want to know
how the locals live," said Miles.

**So here it is:
100 ways to conquer Key West
and look like you live here –
without getting voted off the island.**

Don't just visit; live it.

Do...

Make yourself at home.

We're genuinely glad you're here
and will do our best to show you
a great time.

Don't...

Misspell Ernest Hemingway or Jimmy Buffett.

One "m" in Hemingway;
two "t"s in Buffett.
Don't let it happen again.

Do...

Park in the shade.
Always.

Even if means a longer walk. Trust us.
You haven't known heat until it pours
out of your car in visible waves.

Don't...

Forget to lock your bike – always and everywhere.

Key West is a safe city,
but it's not Disney World.
Bikes disappear like ice cubes in August.

And you won't get any sympathy from anyone,
including the cops, if it wasn't locked when you
leaned it against that parking meter on Duval
Street.

Do...

Attend a drag show – and let yourself enjoy it.

Unless you're an ignorant, insignificant, small-minded knuckle-dragger who will ruin it for everyone.

But do look into the show's content before taking your parents or elderly and easily offended aunt with the heart condition.

Do…

Release any fish
you're not going to eat.

Do...

Ask a bartender
for a "go cup" or "plastic."

Yes, local custom is to take your adult beverage
with you as long as it's in an unmarked plastic cup.
Not a can, not a bottle, a cup.

But finish the drink before
entering your next destination.
Do you bring your own food to a restaurant?

Don't...

Misuse the
"go cup" privilege.

Technically, it's illegal to have an open container of
alcohol in public.
But unmarked plastic cups are generally accepted,
unless you give the police a reason
to investigate the contents.

Don't be the idiot who ruins it
for the rest of us.

Do...

Return a homeless person's friendly greeting.

Don't...

Feel obligated to give a homeless person loose change, a dollar or a cigarette.

Don't...

Exaggerate your ability when scuba diving, snorkeling, fishing, renting a scooter, kayaking or parasailing.

Captains, mates, divemasters and rental agents are there to help. Pay attention.
No one likes a pretentious blowhard who's been everywhere and done everything.
So, don't sneer when someone
hands you a life jacket.
And, please, for one second,
just stop talking.

Do...

Read the
Key West Citizen newspaper...

...for a true taste of local issues and colorful characters.

And forgive the shameless self-promotion, but DO check out some of the locals' favorite features: Mandy Miles' Tan Lines column, Rob O'Neal's photos, The Citizens' Voice, Citizen of the Day and The Crime Report.

Do...

Help raise the sails
on a schooner at sunset.

Don't...

Leave Key West until you've spent a day on the water, fishing with Capt. Stan Miles.

(Of course, I may be a tad biased.)

Do...

Wear shoes in the ocean at Fort Zachary Taylor beach.

Yes, sandals or water shoes look silly, but you'll thank us.
The shoreline is riddled with sharp, painful rocks.
The Florida Keys aren't known for their white, sandy beaches or waves, because the coral reef that surrounds the island chain absorbs the wave action that would typically, over millions of years, pound that rock into sand.

Don't....

Try to save a parking spot.
Ever.

Not with a traffic cone, a beach chair,
or your own body.
We locals will run them over – all of them – to park
within a block of our own front door.

Do...

Heed "Residential Parking" signs.

This book will help you *look* like you live here, but you're not there yet.
If you don't *live* here, you can't *park* there.
Oh, and assume someone is watching from a porch and critiquing your parallel parking skills.

Don't...

Request "Margaritaville," the song, unless you're *in* Margaritaville, the bar.

And even there, it won't make you the most popular guy in the place.

If you're going to look like a local, you'll need to expand your Jimmy Buffett repertoire, beyond the "Songs You Know By Heart" greatest hits album. The guy has some genuinely great songs – learn them.

Don't...

Take your 9-year-old to Fantasy Fest, then complain all over Trip Advisor that the event was inappropriate for a child.

It's called Google. Use it.

Do...

Pronounce "conch" correctly.

It's pronounced [*konk*], rhymes with "honk."
Capitalize it when referring to people who were
actually born here.
Lowercase it when describing the mollusk with the
pretty shell.

Don't...

Embarrass yourself
on a rented scooter.

Incessant beeping makes people not like you.
No one will think you live here.
In fact, they'll be glad you don't.

Don't...

Aggravate police officers on Duval Street.

You're not as cute or as funny
as you think.
And our cops have seen it all before.

Don't...

Panic when you see "grilled dolphin" on a local menu.

They're not serving Flipper,
or any of his Atlantic bottlenose brethren.
Dolphin fish, also known as mahi mahi,
is a flaky, delicious and abundant fish around
here.

Do...

Put a light on your bike.

Don't...

Pedal your bike the wrong way down a one-way street without a bike light while hiding drugs in your sock.

You'll get no sympathy here.
You're simply an imbecile who's asking the police to stop, search and arrest you.
Oh, and you'll absolutely end up in The Citizen's ever-popular daily Crime Report.

Do…

Ask your bartender, cab driver or boat captain to recommend bars, restaurants and attractions.

Don't...

Say, "Customs House."

That beautifully restored brick bastion of Key West
history at the foot of Whitehead Street
deserves to have its name said correctly.
It's just "Custom House,"
NOT *Customs* House.

Do …

**Visit the Key West Museum of Art &
History at the *Custom* House for
excellent exhibits exploring
all aspects of Key West's
culture and history.**

Do...

Remember the final "e" in Greene Street.

If you're going to drink in Sloppy Joe's, Capt. Tony's or Shots 'n' Giggles, the least you can do is spell their location correctly when you post photos to Facebook.

Don't...

Stare too hard at some of our shockingly unique-looking individuals.

Yes, some of them are doing it for the attention,
and that's fine.
But others are just being themselves.
Let them.

Don't...

Make snide comments while posing under a Gay Pride flag.

No one thinks you're funny.
We're too busy counting the stereotypes
you're perpetuating – and placing bets
on when you yourself will come
out of the closet.

Don't…

Try to dock a boat for the first time in a crowded marina.

These ill-advised attempts are great entertainment
for everyone else
(unless their boat is anywhere near yours),
but they generally end in frustration,
embarrassment and some minor,
but costly, property damage.

Do...

**Venture off Duval Street
for dinner, drinks, music
and nightly strolls.**

Don't...

**Order a pain-in-the-butt frozen drink
from a bartender who's
four-deep at happy hour.**

Don't...

Mispronounce Southard Street.

It's pronounced [SU-thurd],
rhymes with "smothered."
It's not [SOW-thurd].

Do…

Stop in the middle of the street and wait for a mother hen to cross with her delightful little chicks in tow.

It's one of those charming, little events that makes everyone stop for a moment and smile.

Do...

Keep a rain jacket and sunglasses in the seat of your scooter.

You will inevitably get caught in a short,
but soaking, afternoon downpour,
and raindrops feel like
needles at 30 mph.

Do...

Assume every other driver is out to kill you when you're on a scooter.

You may be on vacation, but scooters
are not amusement rides.
Pay attention.
Drive sober.
And for God's sake, turn your blinker off.

Do...

Drive the speed limit.

We're not all on vacation.
Some of us have places to be.
So don't crawl down Simonton Street
while holding your Go Pro
out the sunroof.

Don't...

Drive a scooter if you're too nervous to go at least the speed limit.

Contrary to popular belief, traveling timidly
at 12 mph along the side of the road,
encouraging SUVs to pass you
is NOT a safer way to travel.
You *could* get hurt.
You *will* get yelled at.

Do...

Aim for the window seat in the corner of the Green Parrot Bar.

There's always a breeze.

Do…

Watch a sunset
from Fort Zachary Taylor.

Obviously, Mallory Square puts on
a great, nightly Sunset Celebration,
but venture off the beaten path
one evening.

Do...

Make a point to notice a stunning sunset, no matter how long you've been here.

Don't...

Get drunk and fight.

No one is impressed.
Ever.

Do...

Check out the historic U.S. Coast Guard Cutter INGHAM at Truman Waterfront.

It was used in World War II and is now a floating museum, offering daily tours and sunset happy hours on the weekend.

Do...

Attend a movie or special event at the Tropic Cinema.

It's a fantastic movie theater —
and the snack bar sells beer and wine.
(Of course they do, it's Key West)

Do...

Fish from a pier.

But don't throw fishing line in the water.
(Turtles get tangled.)

Don't...

**Believe anyone who says you
can see the lights of Havana
from the Southernmost Point.**

Cuba is 90 miles away
and the Earth is round, genius.

Do...

Listen carefully to instructions when renting a boat.

Key West is surrounded by tricky
and unpredictably shallow water.
You *will* run aground
and you *will* be charged
a boatload for propeller damage.

Do...

Watch where you step at the Key West Butterfly & Nature Conservatory.

Butterflies like to hang out
on the cobblestone pathways.
Please don't squish them.
They live here, too.

Do...

Savor our occasional chilly nights.

Bust out your favorite scarf or buy
a new sweatshirt, then warm up
at Schooner Wharf Bar,
where outdoor heaters provide
the best of both worlds.

Do...

Learn what the locals call
The Conch Republic Seafood Co.

We call it the Conch Farm.
Always have; probably always will.

Do...

Play bocce
at Turtle Kraals restaurant.

It's free for customers, no experience necessary,
and a guaranteed good time.

Do...

Visit the Key West Turtle Museum.

You'll learn that before it was
the name of a waterfront restaurant,
a "turtle kraal," was a holding pen in the harbor
for ill-fated sea turtles.
You'll learn about the turtle-fishing
industry – and ongoing efforts
to protect the amazing creatures.

Do...

Order a "Cuban mix" from a Cuban coffee shop.

It's a popular lunch meat sandwich served on crispy, pressed Cuban bread.

Don't...

Tap on the glass of fish tanks in restaurants, bars, aquariums or art galleries.

How old are you? Seven?
It's just mean.

Do...

Attend a book-signing, lecture, stage performance or gallery opening.

A little culture
never hurt anyone.
(And drinks are available
at all of the above.)

Do...

Visit
Dry Tortugas National Park.

Take the tour of the isolated
Civil War-era Fort Jefferson
and snorkel around the pilings.

Do...

Immerse yourself.

Key West dangles at the blue-green intersection
of Atlantic, Gulf and Caribbean.
Get in or on the water
as often as possible.
Pool's open.

Do...

Learn to parallel park under pressure.

Do...

Behave as if your parents, spouse, boss, children and neighbors are watching your vacation antics.

Because they are.
Or at least they could be.
Most downtown bars have
at least one webcam, live streaming
your bar-dancing adventures to the world.
And this isn't Vegas.
What happens in Key West...
stays on You Tube.

Do...

Learn the story
of the Conch Republic.

Sure it was more publicity stunt
than political strategy, but it's
a true story of government overreach,
the War on Drugs, illegal searches
and a roadblock at the top of the Keys
that brought traffic – and tourism –
to a halt in the 1980s.

Don't...

Order "square grouper" at a restaurant.

It's the difference between
a fish and a felony.
A square grouper is a bale, or bundle,
of pot that's found floating
in the ocean or washed ashore.
The term originated in the 1970s,
when pot smuggling was a popular
"enterprise" in the Florida Keys.

Nowadays, The Square Grouper
is also a fantastic restaurant and bar on
Summerland Key.

Do...

Visit West Martello Tower
at Higgs Beach.

The red brick Civil War fort is now home
to the Key West Garden Club,
a stunning oasis of palm trees, orchids,
banyan trees and cobblestone pathways.
Admission is free, but donations
are gratefully accepted.
Throw 5 or 10 bucks into the donation box.
You won't be sorry.

Do...

Ride a bike whenever possible.

Key West is a flat, easy ride.
And it's much easier to park a bike
than a car in Old Town.

Do...

Locate the closest
Fausto's grocery store.

The local grocery store prides itself
on being,
"Not just a grocery, but a social center."
And it is.
With two downtown locations,
expect to see at least one familiar face
on every visit.

Do...

Let your heart pound at the thought of finding $400 million in gold and silver treasure on the ocean floor.

It happened here in 1985.
Treasure hunter Mel Fisher and his
"Golden Crew" of divers and researchers
found the "mother lode" of treasure from the
Nuestra Senora de Atocha, a Spanish galleon
that sank in a hurricane
off Key West in 1622.

Don't...

Miss out on the
Mel Fisher Maritime Museum.

In addition to true tales of treasure,
the museum hosts intriguing
special events, lectures
and ever-changing exhibits.

Do...

Recognize our local
305 area code.

The area code covers the Keys
And parts of Miami, but we're a bit
like New Yorkers down here
with our fondness for an area code.

Do...

Share mangoes from your tree.

Don't...

Steal someone else's mangoes.

People are generous.
Wait 'til they're offered.

Do...

**Hunt for ghosts
and explore Old Town with
David Sloan's
Key West Ghost Hunt.**

David's also a pretty great writer.
Find his and other books by great local authors at
Key West Island Books on Fleming Street.

Do...

Take a train or trolley tour.

It's a great introduction to the
island's history, architecture, landmarks,
culture and characters.

Don't...

**Snap your fingers, clap your hands
or yell, "Hey, buddy!"
to get a bartender's attention.**

The louder you are,
the more invisible you become.

Do...

Start a collection of beer koozies and insulated cups.

You'll need them in our humidity.

Don't...

Say, "It's 5 o' clock somewhere," every time you drink during the day.

Actually, don't say it at all.
It's no longer clever or original.

Don't...

**Show up early to a yard sale.
Ever.**

Do...

Attend a free outdoor movie at Ibis Bay or Bayview Park.

And while at Ibis Bay, check out
the Dock to Dish
local seafood program.

Don't...

Try to walk to or from the airport unless you can see it from your hotel.

It's farther, and your luggage
is heavier, than you think.
Think taxi.

Don't...

Strap a surfboard to the roof of your Jeep to come to an island with no waves.

Again, it's called Google. Use it.
The same coral reef that gives us some
of the world's best fishing and diving also
takes away our wave action.

Don't...

Wear impossibly high heels on historically uneven sidewalks.

Unless you want to find out
just how good
our local orthopedists are.

Do...

Switch from booze to water at least five hours before *any* boat trip.

A day on the water is more fun
for everyone when you're not
heaving over the side,
praying for it all to be over.

Don't...

Wait 'til you're seasick
to take Dramamine.

By then it's too late; you're screwed.
And you're at the mercy of a captain
who may or may not feel compelled
to tell you that the only cure for seasickness
is to sit under a tree.

Don't...

Spend your whole vacation looking at your phone and posting Facebook photos.

Do...

**Nap in a hammock
whenever possible.**

Do...

**Let a local introduce you
to the sweet, summer flavor
of Spanish limes.**

Don't...

**Book a room on Duval Street
or next to the airport,
and then complain about noise.**

Don't...

Whine about a locals' discount everywhere you go.

Your residency should be recognized
by others, not advertised by you.
It'll happen in due time.
In the meantime, let it go.
The entire bar will think you're
an obnoxious wanna-be,
but hey, at least you saved
60 cents on a drink.

Don't...

Mouth off to bouncers, bartenders or cops.

You won't win.
They're usually bigger than you
And always more sober.

Don't...

**Wear only body paint
at Fantasy Fest, then complain
about the camera-toting pervs
taking your picture.**

Don't...

Go overboard
to prove you're straight.

Exactly who are you trying to convince?

Do...

**Ask permission before
photographing Robert the Doll
at East Martello Museum.**

Do...

Check with the
tow companies before
reporting your car stolen.

It's always a good idea to look for your car
one block in each direction.
Chances are you're just
on the wrong street.

Do...

**Bookmark the
Monroe County Sheriff's Office
website on your phone or computer.
(keysso.net)**

You'll never forget the first time
you see the online mugshot
of someone you know.

Don't...

Waste your Citizen of the Day moment in The Citizen newspaper by saying you enjoy the people and weather of Key West.

Be memorable and creative.
But not negative.

Do...

Learn our major landmarks.

Start with the obvious:
Ernest Hemingway Home & Museum, Truman's
Little White House, Key West Lighthouse,
Mel Fisher Maritime Museum, Mallory Square,
Historic Seaport, Charter Boat Row.

These next ones are a little more obscure.
But no one said looking like a local would be easy:
Key West AIDS Memorial, Old City Hall,
Key West Firehouse Museum, East and West
Martello, City Cemetery, Bayview Park, Douglass
Gym, Key West Africans Memorial, San Carlos
Institute and White Street Pier

Do...

Light a candle
at the grotto at the
Basilica of St. Mary Star of the Sea.

According to local legend, as long as
the grotto stands, Key West will never again
feel the direct force of a hurricane.

Do...

Figure out what a "bight" is.

Bight, which rhymes with sight,
Is another word for bay.
No idea what the city fathers had against
the word everyone else uses,
but Key West has two of them.
Garrison Bight is along
North Roosevelt Boulevard.
Key West Bight is the Historic Seaport.

Don't...

Expect roosters to crow only at daybreak.

They're not real bright,
and they certainly can't tell time.
But at least they'll cock-a-doodle-do
all night long; usually from
just below your bedroom window.
So we've got that going for us.

Don't...

Assume everyone is on vacation.

Do...

Learn the names and general location of our island neighborhoods.

Start with:
Old Town, New Town, Casa Marina district,
Bahama Village, The Meadows,
Upper Duval, Lower Duval
and Truman Annex.

Do...

Heed traffic lights
when walking downtown.

Red means stop;
just like in your town.

Do...

Recycle.

Paper, cardboard, bottles, cans
and any plastic marked with
a number (1 through 10)
on the bottom.

And finally...

Don't...

Get voted off the island!